Your home is ten times more likely to
have a fire than

Pound for Pound, hamburgers cost
more than new cars!

A peanut is not a nut. It is a legume.

Australia's Great Barrier Reef is 1,250
miles long!

Dirty snow melts faster than clean.

The placement of a donkey's eyes in its head enables it to see all four feet at all times!

More people have seen David Copperfield perform live than any other performer in the world.

Albert Einstein was offered the presidency of Israel in 1952, but he declined.

A hedgehog's heart beats 300 times a minute on average!

It takes 17 muscles to smile, 43 to frown.

It is illegal to purchase or consume Jack Daniel's Whiskey in the town in which it is produced!

Girls have more tastebuds than boys.

The octopus' testicles are located in its head.

Beavers can swim half a mile underwater on one gulp of air.

Elephants, lions, and camels roamed Alaska 12,000 years ago.

Chained dogs are 3 times more likely to bite than unchained dogs.

Cleopatra wasn't Egyptian; she was Greek.

The first telephone book was one page long and had only 50 names in it.

Americans eat nearly 100 acres of pizza every day - that's approximately 350 slices per second!

The filming of the movie 'Titanic' cost more than the Titanic itself!

Harry S. Truman was the last U.S. President with no college degree.

15 percent of Americans secretly bite their toes.

Tablecloths were originally meant to serve as towels with which guests could wipe their hands and faces after dinner.

Natural gas has no smell. The odor is artificially added so that people will be able to identify leaks and take measures to stop them.

Bob Hope and Billy Joel were both once boxers.

10 percent of the Russian government's income comes from the sale of vodka.

Extremely high pressured water can easily cut through a steel beam.

English novelist Arnold Bennett drank a glass of water in a Paris Hotel to prove it was safe. He died two months later of Typhoid!

A blue whale's aorta (the main blood vessel) is large enough for a human to crawl through.

Most burglaries occur during the daytime!

Cashew nut shells contain oil that is extremely irritating to human skin.

The streets of Victor, Colorado, once a gold rush town, are paved with low-grade gold.

According to scientific studies, a rat's performance in a maze can be improved by playing music written by Mozart.

The hyoid bone is the only bone in the human body that is not connected to any other bones. It is uniquely shaped "U" and connected by only ligaments and muscles. It in fact acts as a site of attachment for many muscles in the neck.

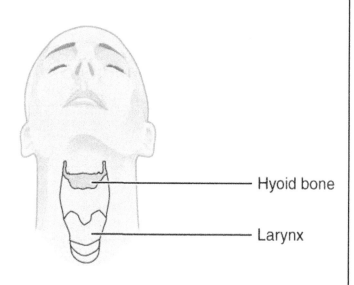

— Hyoid bone

— Larynx

If you were to roll a lung from a human body and out flat, it would be the size of a tennis court.

Only 55% of Americans know that the sun is a star.

On average, women can hear better than men.

In older people, memory is best early in the morning and then declines during the late afternoon.

In Australia, Burger King is called Hungry Jack's.

China has more English speakers than the United States.

A quarter has 119 grooves on its edge, a dime has one less groove!

At birth, a panda bear is smaller than a mouse.

John F. Kennedy was the first Roman Catholic President of the USA!

Babies start dreaming even before they're born.

Babies' eyes do not produce tears until the baby is approximately six to eight weeks old.

Approximately 25,000 workers died during the building of the Panama Canal, and approximately 20,000 of them contracted malaria and yellow fever.

Saturn's rings are about 500,000 miles in circumference but only about a foot thick.

The Greek National anthem has 158 verses!

Because metal was scarce; the Oscars given out during World War II were made of plaster.

The state of Florida is bigger than England.

Human teeth are just as strong as shark teeth.

In the great fire of London, in 1666, half of London was burnt down but only 6 people were injured.

If a pregnant mother suffers organ damage during the pregnancy, the fetus can send stem cells that can cross blood-brain and placental barriers and help repair the damage.

Your mouth produces more saliva before we vomit to protect our teeth from erosion. The acidity in vomit is enough to wear them down.

Gastrocolic reflex causes our body to make room for more food and ramp up colon activity when we eat by taking cues from stomach stretching and digestion. This makes you want to poop after a meal.

Unlike adults, babies can drink and breathe at the same time. For the first three months of life, the larynx sits up high in the nasal cavity, acting as a little snorkel.

A mutation in the LRP5 gene can cause the bone density to be eight times higher than the average, filling life with inconveniences such as sinking like a rock when trying to swim or triumphs like walking away from automobile accidents without a single fracture.

Contrary to popular belief, the white spots on nails are not an indicator of deficiency or excess of calcium and zinc or other vitamins in the diet. In fact, they are commonly caused by minor injuries to the base of the nails.

When electrocuted, people are sometimes thrown far distances. This is caused by the sudden and violent muscle contractions and not the result of the shock.

Pus is primarily white blood cells that died fighting off infection. It also consists of dead or living bacteria (or other microorganisms), and tissue debris.

A feeling of thirst occurs when water loss is equal to 1% of your body weight. The loss of more than 5% can cause fainting, and more than 10% causes death from dehydration.

If you pour warm water into a person's ear, their eyes will move towards that ear, and if you pour cold water into their ear, their eyes will move in the direction of the opposite ear. This is a medical test called "caloric stimulation" and is used to test brain damage.

When you're nervous or crying, you may realize that your throat hurts. You might also feel tightness, a lump in your throat, or have trouble swallowing. This is your body's response to stress. It expands the glottis to provide you with more oxygen.

The heart has its own "little brain," or "intrinsic cardiac nervous system." This "heart brain" is composed of about 40,000 neurons that are similar to the neurons in the brain. This means that the heart has its own nervous system.

Children have more energy than well-trained endurance athletes. They have muscles that are resistant to fatigue, and they also recover faster than both untrained and trained adults.

Infants are born with approximately 300 bones, but as they grow some of these bones fuse together. By the time they reach adulthood, they only have 206 bones.

There is anywhere between 60,000-100,000 miles of blood vessels in the human body. If they were taken out and laid end-to-end, they would be long enough to travel around the world more than three times.

More than half of your bones are located in the hands, wrists, feet, and ankles.

About 60% of your body is made up of water.

Pound for pound, your bones are stronger than steel. A block of bone the size of a matchbox can support up to 18,000 pounds of weight.

A passionate kiss causes the same chemical reactions in the brain that skydiving and firing a gun do.

humans are the best at long-distance runners among animals. Our long legs, upright posture, and ability to shed heat via sweat are all factors that make us good runners. Early humans used to hunt their prey by chasing it for long periods of time until the animals literally died from exhaustion, a technique known as persistence hunting.

Goose bumps evolved to make our ancestors' hair stand up, making them appear more threatening to predators.

Scientists aren't exactly sure why we yawn, but it may help regulate body temperature.

Humans are the only animals with chins.

As you breathe, most of the air is going in and out of one nostril. Every few hours, the workload shifts to the other nostril.

The human nose can detect about 1 trillion smells.

Blood makes up about 8 percent of your total body weight.

You have two kidneys, but only one is necessary to live.

The satisfying sound of cracking your knuckles comes from gas bubbles bursting in your joints.

Thumbs have their own pulse.

Skin is the body's largest organ and can comprise 15 percent of a person's total weight.

Your tongue is made up of eight interwoven muscles, similar in structure to an elephant's trunk or an octopus's tentacle.

On a genetic level, all human beings are more than 99 percent identical.

The foot is one of the most ticklish parts of the body.

Children grow faster in the spring.

Extraocular muscles in the eye are the body's fastest muscles. They allow both of your eyes to flick in the same direction in a single 50-millisecond movement.

The pineal gland, which secretes the hormone melatonin, got its name from its shape, which resembles a pine nut.

Hair grows fast—about 6 inches per year. The only thing in the body that grows faster is bone marrow.

No one really knows what fingerprints are for, but they might help wick water away from our hands, prevent blisters, or improve touch.

The heart beats more than 3 billion times in the average human lifespan.

Blushing is caused by a rush of adrenaline.

Bodies give off a tiny amount of light that's too weak for the eye to see.

Your mouth produces about one liter of saliva each day!

Your brain is sometimes more active when you're asleep than when you're awake.

Your brain is sometimes more active when you're asleep than when you're awake.

The average person has 67 different species of bacteria in their belly button.

You lose about 4kg of skin cells every year!

Your left lung is about 10 percent smaller than your right one.

Nerve impulses sent from the brain move at a speed of 274 km/h.

The only part of the body that has no blood supply is the cornea of the eye. It receives oxygen directly from the air.

The Eiffel Tower was originally intended for Barcelona.

The Eiffel Tower took exactly 2 years, 2 months, and 5 days to create.

The human brain has a memory capacity that is the equivalent of more than four terabytes on a hard drive.

A single human brain generates more electrical impulses in a day than all the telephones of the world combined.

About two-thirds of people tilt their head to the right when kissing.

The average human body contains enough sulfur to kill all the fleas on the average dog, enough carbon to make 900 pencils, enough potassium to fire a toy cannon, enough fat to make seven bars of soap, and enough water to fill a 50-liter barrel.

The human embryo acquires fingerprints within three months of conception.

At least 700 enzymes are active in the human body.

Human beings are the only living things that sleep on their backs.

The average four-year-old child asks 450 questions a day.

Not only human beings, but also koalas have unique fingerprints.

Teeth are the only part of the human body that cannot heal themselves.

On average, a person needs seven minutes to fall asleep.

Right-handed people chew most of their food on the right side of their mouth, whereas left-handed people do so on the left.

The fragrance of apples and bananas can help a person to lose weight.

From 1953 to 1957, NBC's Today Show had a chimpanzee co-host named J. Fred Muggs. It is estimated he brought in the network around $100 million.

If allowed to grow for their whole lifetime, the length of someone's hair would be about 725 kilometers.

Out of all the people who can move their ears, only one-third of them can move just one ear.

The total weight of the bacteria in the human body is 2 kg.

99% of the calcium contained in the human body is in one's teeth.

Human lips are hundreds of times more sensitive than the tips of a person's fingers.

A kiss increases a person's pulse to 100 beats per minute or more.

The total strength of masticatory muscles on one side of your jaw is equal to 195 kilograms.

There are more than 100 different viruses that cause a cold.

If you collected all the iron contained in the human body, you would get just a small cog, big enough only for use in your watch.

You can lose 150 calories per hour if you hit your head against the wall.

A person passes on 278 different types of bacteria to another person when they kiss them. Fortunately, 95% of them are not harmful.

If someone kisses another person for a certain amount of time, this is much more effective in terms of hygiene than using chewing gum, as it normalizes the level of acidity in your oral cavities.

Human beings are the only animals which can draw straight lines.

Human skin is completely replaced about 1,000 times during a person's lifetime.

An animal's yawn based on how large their brain is. The bigger the brain, the longer they will yawn.

A person who smokes a pack of cigarettes a day is doing the equivalent of drinking half a cup of tar a year.

Women blink about two times less often than men.

Men are officially classified as dwarves if their height is below 1.3 m, whereas for women the measure is 1.2 m.

Fingernails grow about four times faster than your toenails.

People with blue eyes are more sensitive to pain than others.

100,000 chemical reactions occur in the human brain every second.

Everyone has dimples on their lower back, but on some people they are more pronounced than on others. They appear where the pelvis joins with the sacrum, so their appearance makes sense.

If one identical twins lacks a certain tooth, the other twin will not have that tooth either.

During a person's lifetime, they spend about 2 weeks kissing.

The facial hair of a blonde-haired man grows faster than that of a man with dark hair.

The strongest muscle in the human body is the tongue.

Leukocytes in the human body live for two to four days, and erythrocytes for three to four months.

The human heart is approximately equal in size to that of a person's fist. An adult's heart weighs 220-260 grams.

Your right lung can take in more air than your left.

The smallest cells in a man's body are sperm cells.

There are more than 70 species of mushrooms that glow in the dark.

At birth, there are 14 billion cells in the human brain. This number does not increase throughout a person's lifetime. After 25 years, the number of cells falls by 100,000 every day. About 70 cells die in the minute it takes you to read a page in a book. After 40 years, the decline of the brain accelerates sharply, and after 50 years neurons (that is, nerve cells) shrink and the brain gets smaller.

An adult person performs around 23,000 inhalations and exhalations a day.

During a person's lifetime, the small intestine is about 2.5 meters. After they die, the muscles in the walls of their intestine relax, and it's length increases to 6 meters.

There are about 40,000 bacteria in the human mouth.

Each of us has around 2,000 taste buds.

The human eye can distinguish 10 million different colors.

The chemical compound in the body which causes feelings of ecstasy (phenylethylamine) is also contained in chocolate. The chemical compound in the body which causes feelings of ecstasy (phenylethylamine) is also contained in chocolate.

The human heart pumps blood at such pressure that it would be able to raise blood up to the fourth floor of a building.

A person burns more calories when they are asleep than when they watch TV.

Every year more than 2 million left-handed people die because of mistakes they make when using machines designed for right-handed people.

By the age of 60 most people lose half of their taste buds.

There is a town in India called Santa Claus

The rate at which a person's hair grows doubles during an airplane flight.

One percent of people can see infrared light and 1% can see ultraviolet radiation.

If you were locked in a completely sealed room, you would not die due to a lack of air, but from carbon dioxide poisoning.

Statistically, only one person out of two billion reaches the age of 116 years old.

On average, a person says 4,800 words in 24 hours.

The retinas inside the eye cover about 650 square mm and contain 137 million light-sensitive cells: 130 million are for black and white vision and 7 million are for helping you see in color.

Our eyes remain the same size as they were at birth, but our nose and ears never stop growing.

In the morning, a person is about 8 millimeters taller than in the evening.

The muscles which help your eyes to focus completes around 100,000 movements a day. In order to make your leg muscles do the same amount of movements, you would need to walk 80 kilometers.

A cough amounts to an explosive charge of air which moves at speeds up to 60 miles per hour.

According to German researchers, the risk of having heart attack is higher on Monday than on any other day of the week.

Bones are about 5 times stronger than steel.

It is impossible to sneeze with your eyes open.

Ingrown toenails are hereditary.

Jousting is the official sport in the state of Maryland.

A person would die quicker from a total lack of sleep than from hunger. Death would occur after ten days without sleep, whereas from hunger it would take several weeks.

Octopuses and squid have three hearts.

Blue whale tongues can weigh as much as an elephant.

Queen Elizabeth's cows sleep on waterbeds.

British military tanks are equipped to make tea.

You can see four states from the top of Chicago's Willis Tower.

Scotland has more than 400 words and expressions for snow.

Cucumber slices can fight bad breath.

The last letter added to the alphabet was actually "J".

Humans have been performing dentistry since 7000 BC, which makes dentists one of the oldest professions.

The first-ever documented feature film was made in Australia in 1906.

Scotland wanted to replicate the Parthenon bigger and cheaper in 1826. It was never completed and is now nicknamed "Scotland's Disgrace".

Snakes can help predict earthquakes. They can sense a coming earthquake from 75 miles away, up to five days before it happens.

People in North Korea are legally only allowed to have one of 28 haircuts. Men and women can choose from 14 different styles.

Another term for your nieces or nephews would be "niblings".

Apples, peaches, and raspberries are all members of the rose family.

Canada eats more macaroni and cheese than any other nation in the world.

The mayor of Talkeetna, Alaska from July 1997 until his death was a cat named Stubbs!

In Switzerland, it is illegal to own just one guinea pig. This is because they are social animals, and considered victims of abuse if they are alone.

Surgeons who play video games at least 3 hours a week perform 27% faster and make 37% fewer errors.

When cellophane was invented in 1908, it was originally intended to be used to protect tablecloths from wine spills.

In the 1980s, Fredric Baur, the founder of Pringles, requested to be buried in a Pringles can. His children honored the request.

You can now get a headstone with a QR code. Called "Living Headstones", they show pages with photos, video biographies, and comments from loved ones.

The NYPD had a police officer follow Andre the Giant whenever he went out drinking. This was to make sure he didn't get drunk and fall on anyone.

A strawberry is not an actual berry, but a banana is.

Hershey's chocolate syrup, Ritz Crackers, Dum Dums, and Oreos are all vegan.

Camel's milk doesn't curdle.

The sound of a Star Wars lightsaber was created by pairing together the sound of an idle film projector and the buzz from an old TV set.

Your tonsils can grow back if there was tissue left behind during the removal process.

There is an uninhabited island in the Bahamas known as Pig Beach, which is populated entirely by swimming pigs.

Without saliva, humans are unable to taste food.

It snowed in the Sahara desert for 30 minutes on February 18, 1979.

In every scene of Fight Club, there is a Starbucks coffee cup.

In Switzerland, it is illegal to flush the toilet after 10pm

William Shakespeare had a curse engraved on his tombstone to prevent anyone from moving his bones.

On Valentine's Day in South Korea, only women give gifts, not men.

March 3 is known as "What if Cats and Dogs Had Opposable Thumbs Day".

The largest living thing on earth is a big tree called giant sequoia.

Astronauts actually get taller when in space.

In California, you can get a ticket if you're driving too slow.

Kangaroos keep growing until they die.

Elvis was originally blonde. He started dying his hair black for an edgier look. Sometimes, he would touch it up himself using shoe polish.

The fear of vegetables is called Lachanophobia.

Females are better at distinguishing colors, while males excel at tracking fast-moving objects and discerning detail from a distance.

A snail can sleep for 3 years.

Using a hands-free device to talk on the phone while driving is shown to be equally or more dangerous than driving drunk.

Lettuce is a member of the sunflower family.

A group of horses will not go to sleep at the same time – at least one of them will stay awake to look out for the others.

Mob boss, Vincent Gigante, used to wander around New York in his bathrobe to convince the police he was insane and avoid capture.

Some people in Russia think that eating ice cream will keep you warm.

In Utah, birds have the right of way on a highway.

Jellyfish don't age and will never die unless they are killed.

There is an island called "Just Enough Room", where there's just enough room for a tree and a house.

You're not allowed to swear if playing in Wimbledon. Because of this, line judges have to learn curse words in every language.

Originating in Berlin in 2008, aggressive sitting became a sport. You can purchase a special stool for this sport for around 70 dollars.

Canadian law requires citizens to answer a math question when entering sweepstakes.

Neptune was the first planet to be found through mathematical predictions rather than telescopic location.

Crows can remember the faces of individual humans. They can also hold a grudge.

In America, it is a federal crime to use your roommate or friend's Netflix account.

A fungus is more closely related to animals on a genetic level than they are to plants.

Eye of newt, the toe of frog, and wool of bat are just archaic terms for mustard seed, buttercup, and holly leaves.

Pure cocoa can help prevent tooth decay.

In Zimbabwe, it is illegal for citizens to make offensive gestures at a passing car.

There are more stars in space than there are grains of sand on every beach in the world.

Humans cannot walk in a straight line without a visual point. When blindfolded, we will gradually walk in a circle.

Even though smoking has been banned on airplanes, ashtrays are mandatory on every plane. This is for safe disposal in case someone breaks the law.

In Greece, women are not legally allowed to wear high heels or tall hats in the Olympic Stadium.

Selfies now cause more deaths than shark attacks.

Pope Francis used to be a nightclub bouncer.

Allodoxaphobia is the fear of other's opinions.

The U.S. government gave Indiana University $1 million to study memes

Dogs can be allergic to humans.

Someone who has Geomelophagia also has the urge to eat raw potatoes.

!

The most leaves ever found on a clover is 56.

All porcupines float in water.

Peaches are members of the almond family.

The longest one-syllable word is "screeched."

Seals sleep only one and a half minutes at a time.

Pigeons have been trained by the U.S. Coast Guard to spot people lost at sea.

In 1634, tulip bulbs were a form of currency in Holland.

Before mercury, brandy was used to fill thermometers.

You don't have to be a lawyer to be a Supreme Court Justice.

The first person crossed Niagara Falls by tightrope in 1859.

Before 1687, clocks were made with only an hour hand.

Hawaii is the only state with one school district.

Cows give more milk when they listen to music.

There are more French restaurants in New York City than in Paris.

The original recipe for chocolate contained chili powder instead of sugar.

Dim lights reduce your appetite.

China only has one time zone.

In ancient Rome, lemons were used as an antidote to all poisons.

Seventeen tons of gold are made into wedding rings each year in the United States.

No only child has been a U.S. President.

For good luck, Egyptian women pinch the bride on her wedding day.

Ancient Greeks and Romans thought the veil protected the bride from evil spirits. Brides have worn veils ever since.

Engagement and wedding rings are worn on the fourth finger of the left hand because it was once thought that a vein in that finger led directly to the heart.

The marriage of Sheik Rashid Bin Saeed Al Maktoum's son to Princess Salama in Dubai in May 1981 was the most expensive wedding ever. The price tag? $44 million!

In many cultures around the world -- including Celtic, Hindu and Egyptian weddings -- the hands of a bride and groom are literally tied together to demonstrate the couple's commitment to each other and their new bond as a married couple (giving us the popular phrase "tying the knot").

Queen Victoria's wedding cake weighed a whopping 300 pounds.

Greek brides believed that tucking a lump of sugar into the wedding gown would bring sweetness throughout married life.

Some South Koreans believe that in order to make the groom ready for the first night of the marriage, his feet need to be beaten by dead fish and bamboo sticks

🫨

In India, women born under Mangal Dosha (a Hindu astrological combination) are thought to be cursed with bad luck, especially in marriage. In order to remedy this, a kumbh vivah – a ceremony in which the woman marries either a peepal or banana tree or an idol of the god Vishnu – is performed before their actual wedding to break the curse.

During the weddings of Kenya's Maasai people, The father basically spits on his daughter for good luck before she leaves with her new husband.

In Mauritania, brides work towards getting healthier and chubbier. It is believed to be a good luck charm in their tradition. So they go to fat farms to gain weight.

When a man asks for a girl's hand in marriage in Fiji he has to gift a whale's tooth to the father-in-law.

One of the Scotland traditions actually involves family & friends showering the couple with all sorts of disgusting things and then tying her to a tree. This is only done so that the bride & groom can prove that they are ready for anything.

In China, the brides have to cry every day for an hour for a month before their wedding. Other female relatives join in as well. Crying for the Tujia people in China means the welcoming of a good marriage or event.

During a wedding ceremony in Sweden, if a groom leaves the room, all men stand up to kiss the bride and if a bride excuses herself to the bathroom, then all the women line up to kiss the groom.

A groom is required in Wales to gift his new bride with a carved 'Lovespoon' signifying that he will never let her go hungry.

In the Marquesas Islands of French Polynesia, after the wedding is done, the relatives lie down on the ground face down and the couple walks on them as if it were a rug made out of people.

Polterabend is a German wedding custom in which, on the night before the wedding, the guests break porcelain to bring luck to the couple's marriage.

Mothers or elders in certain African tribes accompany the newlyweds on honeymoon to 'educate' them on how to spend the night.

In South Africa, the parents of the bride and groom bring embers and ashes from their own fireplaces, and the newlyweds use those flames from their childhood homes to light their first fire in the hearth of their new home to symbolize the two families coming together as one in blissful matrimony.

At traditional Filipino weddings, the bride and groom make a pair of white doves kiss as they themselves are kissing, and then release the doves into the air as a way of signifying their love for each other and their aspirations of a peaceful and harmonious life together.

Turkish weddings have a henna night, in which the bride is adorned in a red outfit with a red veil draped over her head, and guests place gold coins on her palms on top of a dollop of henna, and sing traditional Turkish songs about leaving her old life and entering her new married life.

LEGO's founder, Ole Kirk Christiansen, created the name "LEGO" by taking the first two letters of the Danish words LEG GODT, meaning "play well".

If you put the 340 million Minifigures produced last year next to each other in a line, it would stretch a whopping 7,900 km – that's almost the distance from London, UK to Beijing, China!

The famous LEGO brick that we play with today is more than 50 years old. The bricks made way back in 1958 will still fit perfectly with those you play with today!

The moulds used to produce LEGO bricks are accurate to within two-thousandth of a millimeter (0.002 mm!). Because of this high degree of accuracy, there are only around 18 bricks in every million produced that fail to meet the company's high quality standard.

The world's tallest LEGO tower is 28.7m high, made from with 465,000 bricks!

LEGO Minifigures are the world's largest population, with over 4 billion of them around the world!

During the Christmas season almost 28 LEGO sets are sold each second.

On average there are 80 LEGO bricks for every person on earth.

At LEGO attractions, such as LEGOLAND Discovery Centre Manchester, people are hired as "Master Model Builders".

Laid end to end, the number of LEGO bricks sold in a year would reach more than five times round the world.

Young women in Japan have, in recent years, been engaging in an orthodontic work known locally as Yaeba "double tooth", to upper canines. It involves having their teeth look a little more crooked than nature as a sign of youthfulness and natural beauty.

In Burma and Thailand, KayanLahwi girls tribe decorates their necks with a series of metal rings. They start wearing these heavy coils when they are just five years old, over time women can have as many as 25 fitted to their necks.

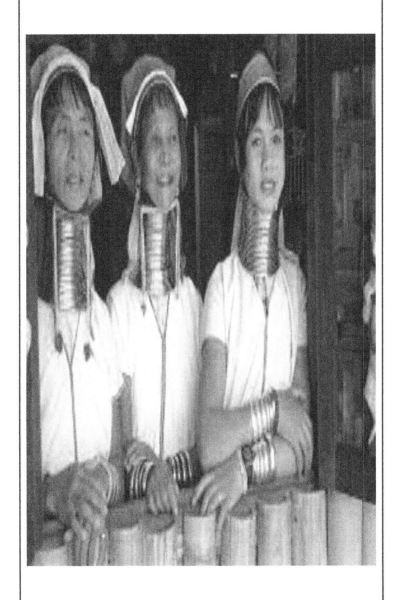

Foot binding was an important part of Chinese culture for centuries, until it was banned in the 1940s. It involved breaking the women's toes before they were bent back against the sole of the foot to be "bound" in place by a tight fabric wrapping. This makes the feet of Chinese women small and delicate as a symbol of status and social standing in rural China, also women who underwent the foot binding procedure were said to make particularly good wives, as they wouldn't complain too much.

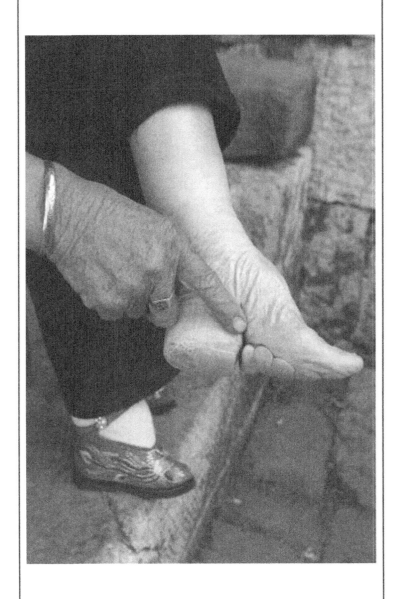

In Africa, the Karo tribe from Ethiopia and South Sudan people mark the faces of teenage boys and girls in the tribe with a knife as a rite of passage. Usually, girls are marked with beautiful patterns, and boys with three parallel lines, which are supposed to represent their entry into manhood. Although the procedure can be painful, Dinka youths are expressly forbidden from crying or even flinching during their own scarification, since doing so would bring shame to their whole family.

For many cultures around the world, tattoos continue to have an enormous cultural significance. The Maori in New Zealand has decorated their skin for centuries with distinctive black and dark blue patterns called Ta-Mako, including facial and lip tattoos. Women will often tattoo their lips blue, while also tattooing Ta-Mako designs on their chin – a sign of true Maori beauty.

Ear stretching, which is still carried out by the Maasai tribe of Kenya, might raise an eyebrow or two. Normally, Maasai women use weights to stretch the earlobes until they are almost long enough to touch the shoulder and combine this with nicely shaved heads.

Thailand seems to be rich in several traditional practices to enhance beauty. One of these is cheek piercing, which may seem horrifying to people living outside Thailand due to the enormous pain endured during the process. For the Thai people, however, this is an act of devotion to themselves, and also a procedure that they believe will help chase evil spirits from their lives. Interestingly, Thai people are deeply rooted in this culture, often performing the ritual during the 10-day vegetarian festival in Phuket. The competition is usually stiff with people using guns, swords, and even bikes, to pierce through their cheeks.

Although no longer practiced, skull binding was once widespread among communities in areas as diverse as Peru and Iraq. Archaeologists have found skulls from about 7,000 BC in Peru, which show elongated skulls, probably achieved by wrapping an infant's head tightly in fabric or even using wooden boards to encourage the skull to grow lengthways as the child gets older. Although it is unclear exactly why skull binding was carried out, there are theories that it was for ritual or symbolic reasons, and that those chosen for the procedure may have had an elevated status in society.

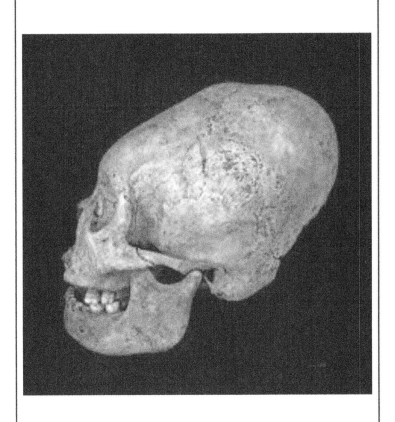

While tattoos may still be frowned upon in some cultures, temporary ink drawings on the hands, body, or face are often used to celebrate special occasions – safe in the knowledge that the images will fade after a few weeks or a few good washes. Henna is used frequently in India to decorate visible parts of the body on a bride's wedding day, or for certain religious festivals throughout the year. Delicate and intricate patterns are painted directly onto the skin to create a beautiful visual effect, a fad that is currently being copied by Western women, who are fascinated by Indian culture, or are just too scared to have a permanent tattoo.

Skin whitening is another modern beauty trend and one that often causes a lot more harm than good. Women in Africa, South America, and particularly Asia, are constantly bombarded by images of white Western women as the beauty ideal. As a consequence, they often turn to unproven and sometimes dangerous skin whitening products in a bid to lighten their own natural skin color. Naturally, a lot of these products contain unpleasant chemicals, which if used incorrectly, or over a long period of time, can burn the skin, leaving it looking damaged and unhealthy. We are now finally witnessing a larger representation of colored women in the media, which is somewhat countering this dangerous craze.

Women in some Indonesian tribes have been going through a painful procedure called teeth chiseling for decades. The procedure leaves the women with smaller, pointed teeth – a sign of a higher social status in this particular tribe. However, teeth chiseling is carried out in other parts of the world for different reasons. In Bali, for example, one tribe files down their teeth to sharp points because they believe their teeth represent anger and hatred, and that they can rid their lives of negative emotions by essentially reducing their teeth. Other cultures, such as the African Wapare tribe, file their teeth to make their warriors look more like animals – and presumably, to look more fearsome on the field of battle.

The women of the Apatani tribe in India are well-known for their unusual nasal decorations – plugs inserted into the side of their nose with the express aim of making them look less attractive. Actually, it is said that the Apatani women were once considered the most beautiful in all of India. However, this beauty came at a price as their villages were constantly being raided by neighboring tribes looking to steal themselves an Apatani bride. And so, the rather ugly and ungainly nose plugs were created, proving to be very successful at keeping men from other tribes away from their women. This practice has continued even into the modern era, though it is now just an Apatani tradition, rather than an unconventional anti-theft device.

Lip plates are worn by women of the Mursi tribe in Ethiopia, in an effort to appear more beautiful and desirable to men looking for a bride. The process of inserting the lip plate starts when a girl reaches puberty. As a normal practice, plates of increasing size are inserted, gradually stretching the lower lip, until she can insert a full-size symbolic lip plate. The plate is often decorated by the woman herself to show off her skills, and an element of her personality, to prospective husbands. More interesting is the fact that there is a definite hierarchy when it comes to the lip plates of the Mursi. If you want to catch the attention of the most powerful men in the village, then you have to be willing to have your lip stretched to accommodate the biggest plate.

In Iran, you will often see young women and men proudly sporting bandages on their noses or other parts of their faces. This is to give the impression that they have undergone plastic surgery, something that is now symbolic of wealth and status in Iranian culture. Sometimes the bandages hide a real nose job, although it may have been carried out weeks before. In other cases, however, no plastic surgery was carried out at all, but young Iranians still want their peers to think that they are wealthy enough to afford such elective procedures – and brave enough to undergo them.

The King of Hearts is the only king in a deck of cards without a mustache

Dreamt is the only word in the English language that ends with "mt."

A Greek-Canadian man invented the "Hawaiian" pizza.

If you open your eyes in a pitch-black room, the color you'll see is called "Eigengrau."

Cats can't taste sweet things because of a genetic defect.

A group of hippos is called a "bloat."

Pogonophobia is the fear of beards.

Alaska is the only state whose name is on one row on a keyboard.

Tesseradecades, "aftercataracts," and "sweaterdresses" are the longest words you can type using only your left hand.

The average adult spends more time on the toilet than they do exercising.

Your fingernails grow faster on your dominant hand.

A "jiffy" is about one trillionth of a second.

Dragonflies have six legs but can't walk.

Golf balls tend to have 336 "dimples."

Montpelier, Vermont, is the only U.S. capital without a McDonald's.

Apple seeds contain cyanide.

Mulan has the highest kill-count of any Disney character.

A cubic inch of human bone can bear the weight of five standard pickup trucks.

A frigate bird can sleep while it flies.

Jupiter is twice as massive as all the other planets combined.

There's a trademark on the world's darkest shade of black.

The chicken and the ostrich are the closest living relatives of the Tyrannosaurus rex.

The average American spends about 2.5 days a year looking for lost items.

If you plug your nose, you can't tell the difference between an apple, a potato, and an onion.

Punctuation wasn't always a part of our written language.

The real name of Monopoly mascot Uncle Pennybags is Milburn Pennybags.

The infinity sign is called a lemniscate.

It's illegal to hunt camels in Arizona.

Malabar giant squirrel in southern India, weighing around four pounds and measuring up to three feet from head to tail.

Spoonfeed is the longest English word with its letters in reverse alphabetical order.

The largest scrambled eggs ever made weighed nearly 3.5 tons and was made in Cundinamarca, Colombia, on 11 October 2019.

There's a city called "Rome" on every continent except Antarctica.

Riding roller coasters can help you pass kidney stones.

Cap'n Crunch's full name is Captain Horatio Magellan Crunch.

The first email was sent by Ray Tomlinson to himself in 1971.

Movie trailers got their name because they were originally shown after the movie.

People used to answer the phone by saying "ahoy" instead of "hello."

Pound cake originally included a pound of all of its ingredients.

Rainbows were called "bows of promise" in Victorian English.

The tool used to measure your feet at the shoe store is called a "Brannock Device."

Space travel makes mice run in loops.

There's an optical illusion at bottom of the sea.

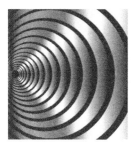

An earthquake might have shrunk Mount Everest.

Queen Elizabeth II is a trained mechanic.

The average American produces 4.5 pounds of trash per day.

One man set a world record by putting on 260 T-shirts at once.

There is only one walled city in North America.

Ravens know when someone is spying on them.

Frank Sinatra was offered the starring role in Die Hard when he was in his 70s.

Sleeping through summer is called "estivation."

The cheesiest pizza ever was topped with 154 varieties of cheese.

Basenji dogs are the only breed that doesn't bark.

The most common password is "123456."

The largest bill to go into circulation in the U.S. was a $10,000 note.

Messages from your brain travel along your nerves at up to 200 miles per hour.

Nobel Prize-winning scientist Marie Curie's 100-year-old belongings are still radioactive.

Most pandas in the world are on loan from China.

The average person has four to six dreams a night.

The sun makes up more than 99 percent of our solar system's mass.

In old Christian art, good angels were red and Satan was blue.

A Harry Potter book filled with typos sold for $90,000.

In 2008, a British teen changed his name to "Captain Fantastic Faster Than Superman Spiderman Batman Wolverine Hulk And The Flash Combined."

The Bubonic plague encouraged Shakespeare to write poetry.

Facial reconstruction was used to see what dogs looked like 4,000 years ago.

Scientists discovered the fossil of a 430-million-year-old monster.

Antarctica is the largest unclaimed territory on Earth.

The ocean is home to nearly 95 percent of all life.

There's enough gold in the ocean for us each to have 9 pounds of it!

Coral produces its own sunscreen.

There's an ice sheet larger than the continental United States.

The planet's longest mountain range is underwater and is 10 times longer than the Andes.

The Pacific is wider than the moon.

One iceberg could supply a million people with drinking water for five years.

Pressure at the bottom of the ocean would crush you like an ant.

Water at the bottom of the ocean is incredibly hot.

The planet's biggest waterfall is in the ocean.

The loudest ocean sound came from an icequake.

Oceans have lakes and rivers too.

More people have been to the moon than to the Mariana Trench.

The Mediterranean used to be a dry basin until some 5 million years ago during the Zanclean flood—in which water from the Atlantic poured through the Strait of Gibraltar and filled the basin.

Most of Earth's volcanic activity happens in the ocean.

Tsunamis move at 500 miles per hour when the ocean depth is 3.7 miles.

The United States lost a hydrogen bomb in the ocean.

The world's largest living structure is the Great Barrier Reef off the coast of Australia. The reef spreads out over an area of 133,000 square miles, and is so huge it can actually be seen from outer space.

There are 3 million shipwrecks in the ocean.

If all the ice melted, the sea level would rise 26 stories.

The ocean is our greatest source of oxygen.

!

The biggest ocean waves are beneath its surface.

The ocean has more artifacts than all the world's museums combined.

Most of the oxygen in our atmosphere comes from tiny marine plants in the ocean.

More than 90 percent of the planet's lifeforms are undiscovered and underwater.

We have better maps of Mars than of the ocean.

Rubber bands last longer when refrigerated.

The Super Soaker was designed and invented by a NASA engineer.

Flamingos can only eat with their heads upside down.

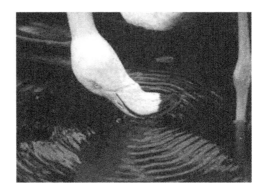

There are only four words in the English language which end in "dous": tremendous, horrendous, stupendous, and hazardous.

There are 32 muscles in a cat's ear.

Salt used to be a currency.

Junk food is as addictive as drugs.

In most advertisements, including newspapers, the time displayed on a watch is 10:10.

Honey is the only food that does not spoil.

A dragonfly has a lifespan of only one day.

Toy Story helped sell the Etch-a-Sketch.

Four out of five children recognize the McDonald's logo at three years old.

One single teaspoon of honey represents the life work of 12 bees.

It's impossible to tickle yourself.

It's impossible for you to lick your own elbow.

Venus is the only planet that rotates clockwise.

3.6 cans of Spam are consumed each second.

The average American looks at eight houses before buying one.

Oreo has made enough cookies to span five back and forth trips to the moon.

A giraffe can go longer without water than a camel can.

Chalk is edible.

Al Capone's business card said he was a used furniture dealer.

The only real person to be a Pez head was Betsy Ross.

Peanuts are one of the ingredients of dynamite.

1 in 200 men in the world are direct descendants of Genghis Khan.

Alfred Hitchcock didn't have a belly button.

A blob of toothpaste is called a nurdle.

Most babies are conceived in December.

Slinkies are 82 feet long.

New Jersey grows two-thirds of the world's eggplants.

Each year, Americans eat enough burgers to circle the earth more than 32 times.

There are 293 ways to make change for a dollar.

You spray 2.5 drops of saliva per word.

A shark is the only animal that can blink both its eyes.

If your stomach doesn't produce a new layer of mucus every two weeks, it will digest itself.

An ostrich's eye is bigger than its brain.

Barbie's full name is Barbara Millicent Roberts.

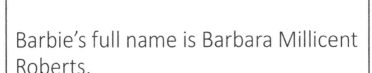

Every time you lick a stamp, you consume one-tenth of a calorie.

The average person falls asleep in seven minutes.

Most American car horns honk in the key of F.

To escape the grip of a crocodile's jaws, push your thumbs into its eyeballs. It will let you go instantly.

More Monopoly money is printed in a year than actual money throughout the world.

Finland has the most metal bands per capita.

According to research, fans of classical music and those who love heavy metal have shown to have similar personalities.

Somali pirates have such a hatred for Western culture, that the British Navy uses music from Britney Spears to scare them off.

Singing in a group boosts morale.

In 1993, Rod Stewart hosted the largest free concert.

In 2015, astronaut Chris Hadfield released an album while still in space.

Metallica is the only band to have played on all seven continents. (Yes, including Antarctica.)

Music has some pretty interesting effects on living things. It makes plants grow faster and cows produce more milk.

In 2016, Mozart sold more CDs than Beyonce.

Prince is credited with playing 27 different instruments on his debut album.

Listening to music can improve your physical performance.

Women make up 70 percent of the population that lives in "absolute poverty." That means they live on less than $1.00 a day to survive.

It's been calculated that the average woman will "eat" about four pounds of lipstick throughout the course of her life.

Women hiccup less than men.

The two highest IQ scores in history both belonged to women.

Studies found that women also have a more heightened sense of smell.

The country of Russia is bigger than Pluto.

!

Many oranges are actually green.

The opposite sides of a die will always add up to seven.

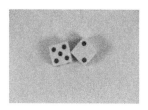

On average, 100 people choke to death on ballpoint pens every year.

It's possible to turn peanut butter into diamonds.

Linda Lou Taylor of Indiana holds the Guinness World Record for the most married person. She's been married 23 times.

The world's most expensive dessert from New York City's Serendipity 3 cafe came in at a whopping $25,000.

Bears don't poop during hibernation.

Animals that lay eggs don't have belly buttons.

Mosquitoes are attracted to people who just ate bananas.

Emus and kangaroos cannot walk backward.

Rhubarb can spring up so fast that you can actually hear it grow.

Due to their high oil content and lower water content, pistachios are prone to self-heating. In fact, if transported in large groups, they can spontaneously combust!

In the Middle Ages, black pepper was considered a luxury. It was even used to pay rent and taxes on occasion.

In 1965, astronaut John Young snuck a corned beef sandwich into space for a six-hour mission.

The oldest known soup recipe dates back to 6,000 B.C. Among the ingredients? Hippopotamus and sparrow meat.

In the 1830s, ketchup was used medicinally.

Space is completely, totally, and utterly silent.

The number of hot dogs consumed on the Fourth of July could stretch from Washington, D.C., to Los Angeles five times over.

No one knows just how many stars are in space.

The footprints made on the moon will be there for 100 million years.

Scientists have found a mass of water vapor cloud 10 billion light-years away from earth that is 140 trillion times the mass of water on Earth's surface.

A NASA spacesuit costs a cool $12,000,000.

Neptune orbits the sun once every 165 years.

What do think of our book?

If you enjoyed this book, we would be very grateful if you could leave us a review.

We would be very happy to receive your suggestions.

Printed in Great Britain
by Amazon